THE FIFTH FIGURE

Jean 'Binta' Breeze is a poet, actress, dancer, choreographer, film writer and theatre director. She has released four other poetry books, *Riddym Ravings* (Race Today), *Spring Cleaning* (Virago), and *On the Edge of an Island* and *The Arrival of Brighteye* (both Bloodaxe), as well as several records, including *Tracks* with the Dennis Bovell Dub Band and *Riding On De Riddym: selected spoken works* (CD from 57 Productions). She has performed her work throughout the world, including tours of the Caribbean, North America, Europe, South East Asia and Africa, and now divides her time between Jamaica and Leicester. She received a NESTA Award in 2003, which assisted her in the writing of her latest book, *The Fifth Figure* (Bloodaxe Books, 2006).

The cover shows a detail from the painting 'Villagers Merrymaking in the Island of St Vincent' (1775) by Agostino Brunias, held by the National Library of Jamaica, and featured on the website http://hitchcock.itc.virginia.edu/Slavery/

JEAN 'BINTA' BREEZE

The Fifth Figure

BLOODAXE BOOKS

ISBN: 1 85224 732 0

First published 2006 by
Bloodaxe Books Ltd,
Highgreen,
Tarset,
Northumberland NE48 1RP.

www.bloodaxebooks.com
For further information about Bloodaxe titles
please visit our website or write to
the above address for a catalogue.

Bloodaxe Books Ltd acknowledges
the financial assistance of
Arts Council England, North East.

ACKNOWLEDGEMENT: This book was written
with the assistance of a grant from NESTA.
NESTA is the National Endowment for Science,
Technology and the Arts, the organisation that
invests in UK creativity and innovation.

Cover printing by J. Thomson Colour Printers Ltd, Glasgow.

Printed in Great Britain by
Bell & Bain Limited, Glasgow, Scotland.

CONTENTS

FIGURE ONE

After my mother and father died,
it was three years before school was done,
going to live with my brother James
seemed like it would be more fun.
He was all I had left as close family,
a missionary in west Jamaica.
Surely, sweet Lord, it would be worthwhile
to serve in a distant land,
for anywhere, away from here,
would surely stop my grieving.

I packed my cases carefully,
cases of white muslin.
James said it was the coolest thing to wear
but even that did not help me prepare
for the heat that slapped me in my face
on my arrival in Jamaica.
The glare was too much for my eyes.
I wore my bonnet over them for shade
so I did not see the mountains
that my brother had declared
so strikingly dramatic
he felt that Zion could be here.
I knew James, from his letters,
had quite fallen for the place,
so I whispered a lonely prayer,
'Lord let me find home here.'

There's nothing like a hug. My God,
how I needed arms around me.
I lay my head on his shoulder, and wept.
He dried my eyes as we started our journey.

All the way across the island
I was eaten up by green.
Lush green like it was burning
where it flowered into red
and the shocking nature of the scenery
left me feeling quite numb.
I, so overwhelmed by colour,
felt completely naked in the sun.

We crossed over the mountains
and descended into cane,
long flat hours of cane
clashing violently with the turquoise of sea,
rising into the gentler hills beyond.

James owned no cane,
he had not come
to the island with money for land,
as a young Anglican vicar
he had left very few choices at home.
He had made a private vow of poverty
and the colonies had wakened his conscience.
In one of the first free villages
in the hills above the cane
the Anglican church had been given some land
and there he had built a home.

He had toiled alongside the native men
building the church from stone
and had bent low under the sun for years,
clutching a garden out of the wild.
As the sun was dying from the skies
this was where I arrived.

They're white. Who are they? They're as white as me though their
skins are reddened, sometimes slightly bronzed by sun.

James said they were the illegitimate children the plantation owners
had fathered with slave women and then given or mostly sold them
their own freedom. This was after church on my first Sunday.

I could not believe it. The women were exquisite, despite the cheap-
ness of their clothes. The men were lithe and seemed too handsome
for the eyes. They stood out even more against the smaller number
who were still completely black.

James thought he'd found the rainbow people
he and his God were looking for,
but I was shocked by the evidence of sin
and the shame that such beauty lacked.

Nana ran the household
and lived in her cottage nearby.
You could see that she was black
but you could also see the white.
They had banded together
and they had made
a village for themselves,
inviting James to read them their rites.
He was so delighted,
introducing me to all,
while I was wondering if he had ever been tempted
by these dark-eyed women in their shawls.

I walked with him and Nana,
through the garden at the back
where all the vegetables we ate were planted
and fruits we would never lack.
That was the first I heard of him,
Nana's son, the one called Gobi,
who had gone into town to market
and was due back later on.

He walked into the dining-room
as we sat down to dinner
and in the midst of Nana's hugs
and James's fervent handshakes,
I looked at the first man in my life
who made it difficult to swallow.
Thick curly black hair and evergreen eyes
and limbs that were made for fine clothing,
skin slightly bronzed,
how he smiled at me
as he took my hand for shaking.
This was all it took to keep me awake
sitting by the window, stargazing
while he told the tales of market
against the sounds of the night
and his voice so soft became for me
the rhythm of the island.

Our first dinner invitation
after I arrived
came from the great house on the plains below.

Apparently they owned all we could see.
James had often been asked as an extra man
but my arrival added a single white woman.
I understood then where the lines were drawn
as Gobi, though the son of the owner,
was a feared embarrassment
who would never be invited
and the legal son was there to entertain us.

Gobi, but with blue eyes.
Our host introduced his son.
Dear God. It is true. This is his history
but blue eyes and skin that reddened
would inherit all the land
and be the host to pure whites in this mansion,
this man now asking me to dance
the first figure of the quadrille
was the only son,
it was written in his stance.
Charles, as he was introduced
took great pleasure being teacher
to me, the newest arrival here
and he turned on all his charms.

First the music to enter,
and take your partner's arm
choosing a cardinal point which would be home.
Then a sweeping curtsey to him
followed by another to the side
honouring the presence of the opposite man,
then balancing
right left right left touch,
left right left right touch
ending the bars with a turn
wheeling with your partner round and round.
Then it had to be repeated
facing another cardinal point.
Oh so simple, I learnt with ease
but I refused the second figure
and made James's side my home.
I could not quite get over
the stiffness of Charles's body
or the familiar face so near my own.

I learnt in a few short weeks here
so many differences
between the village
and the large plantation down below.
Charles now started riding up,
completely unannounced,
as if we and all we owned belonged to him.
His constant rudeness to Nana
I finally understood
and why Gobi would disappear
with anger in his eyes
while James would welcome him formally
with wrinkles in his brow.
I learnt to lower my head and simply sew.

Why didn't I fall in love with Charles?
He was single, he was rich.
Why didn't I feel the need for him
instead of hiding stitch by stitch.
Maybe the magic of the hills,
the spirits in the bush,
were working their charms on all my thoughts.
Maybe I didn't pray enough
and turn my queries to the Lord.
So the church became my solace
as I couldn't share these feelings with James,
I sat in the shade of stone and cross,
I spent hours on my knees.
Before God I laid my needs
and did what I could to please.

I weeded the food garden,
trimmed the roses in front.
I worked in the kitchen with Nana,
learning how she cooked
but everytime Gobi walked in,
I felt like a woman tormented,
I felt like a woman in sin.

It was Nana's idea
that Gobi would teach me to dance,
so they cleared all the living-room furniture,
and I almost fell in his arms.

The difference in how Gobi held me,
his hand on my hip, not on my back,
while Nana beat out the rhythm
and James tried to sing as he clapped.

It was almost the same as the quadrille,
but the beat had a pulse I could find.
It did something strange in the pelvis
and I found my hips moving, entwined.
I broke off as soon as I was able,
my face bright red from his touch
and James, I felt, in that moment,
thought that it was enough.
Something he saw in my face then,
made him think that I wasn't prepared,
to be so exposed to male talent,
so he helped me to close down that door.
From then I could see he was worried,
so I laughed and made it a joke,
about how we the English just stiffened
and embarrassed ourselves on the floor.

That dance proved a dangerous moment,
and I couldn't forget though I tried,
how Gobi's arms felt wrapped around me,
though my mind told my heart that I lied.
I now started avoiding his company,
which was obvious to Nana and James,
but Gobi seemed so disheartened,
I thought my own rudeness insane.
Nana, in one of her proverbial moments,
said that spirits had a will of their own
and although we tried to avoid it,
she'd seen love flower in more dangerous ground.
It was then that she started to tell me
the truth of Gobi's father and her
and why he gave them their freedom
though he couldn't recognise him as son.

Just looking at Nana you could see
how beautiful she must have been,
for he moved her out of the field gang
and installed her in the kitchen.

At the time his wife was just pregnant
and had locked him out of her room
and he was spending his evenings in the kitchen,
nursing a bottle of rum.
While Nana cleaned up around him
he started teaching her sailors' songs.
After a while he would pour her a drink,
she started dancing while he sang along
so it wasn't strange that before very long
they ended up in each other's arms
and two sons were born in the great house
without many months between them.
It would have been very embarrassing
keeping both
so he gave her some land,
land he was selling in the mountains,
land that was no use for cane.
That's when Nana took up church duties
and when James came along
she offered to be his housekeeper
if he would educate her son.
James was a wonderful teacher
and Gobi learnt easily,
so together they started a village school
encouraging children to come.
The two of them taught together
and Nana was mother to both.
This was just at the end of slavery
I was there when Freedom came.

'Jubilee, Jubilee,
this is the year of Jubilee,
Queen Victoria set me free,
Queen Victoria set me free.'

The village sang and danced all night
And that was when it started.

I let him touch me   dear God, I let him in   and now he's gone
I let him touch me   I let the bushes rule my mind   James
wouldn't let us marry   I tried   I really tried   but all our walks
by the river   it felt like my body wasn't mine   I let him hold me
and we couldn't stop   dear God we couldn't stop   I felt his arms
around me and   I wanted him all   I wanted him all and I swear
it was the bushes   oh god   it was the bushes   I let him touch
me   then I let him in   and I knew   I knew dear God   that it
was sin   but the pleasure of his nearness   the warmth beneath
my waist   the feeling of his fingers   as they brushed against
my breast   I felt I was a mermaid   and I pulled him in   into
my dark waters   Gobi   I called his name loud   as I let his
hardness in   nothing mattered in that moment   but our coming
Gobi   I screamed out   as I felt the waters burst inside me
and I saw his head explode   and blood was all around me and
Charles   was mounted on his horse   above us   on the banking
the smoking gun   Nooooo!   Dear God   nooooo!   My last
scream   Charles's laughter.

Rape, they said, Rape   that was the jurisdiction   and I couldn't
look at Nana   she knew that they were lying   Rape
freedom couldn't change the verdict   he was black   and I was
white   nothing had changed really

But I knew it was the bushes   black magic in the bushes   I knew
there would be no escape   from the magic of the bushes   I sat
there numb   with no escape   the house was all surrounded
I sat in the window   I would have to keep guard   keep away
the bushes   I kept a machete   by the chair   if they ever came
any nearer   I knew what I would have to do   chop them
chop them   chop away the bushes   I sat there watching
all those months   while my belly kept on growing   he's still
inside me   he's growing inside me   how could I look at James
how could I look at Nana   there would be more blood soon
there would be more blood from inside   and the child   what if
the child came black   what if the child had his eyes   I would
never look at the child   and soon   soon   it would be here

Nana gathered hot water and moved me to my bed   the bushes
would take over   now I was not there to watch them   the child
kept moving further down   it was intent on coming Nana guided
the child and wrapped it in the blanket

No take it away now give it to the bushes I was screaming
give it to the bushes the bush will claim its own James was
trying to hold me down as Nana cleaned the blood below me
a girl he said a girl surely you want to hold the child you
need to give it milk give it bush tea give it Nana's bush tea
it's not mine it came in from the bushes it's not mine feed it
from the bushes and then the weight descended and I slept.

For a moment I didn't know where I was. The sun was warm on
my face through the window, Nana brought tea and I slept

I woke again. The moon against the banyan tree. Nana brought food
and I ate. Nana brought more tea. I slept.
 Just keep bringing me more tea, let me sleep.
 I woke to the church bell next morning. Nana brought in the
child. The sun shattered into fine pieces. The memories came back
from the wild. Bush baby. Bush baby. I screamed and the window
shattered and the bush entered filling the room. I ran to the chair
by the window next door where I knew I had some control. The
machete. The machete. Where is the machete? The bush is coming
in. Don't bring the child near me She's letting in the bush. She's
letting in the bush.

I will not move from this window. I will not suckle the child. I will
not let the bush in. I will live here till I die.

Nana brings me soup every afternoon, and now she knows what I
have to do, she stands in the window with the machete while I
take a bath. I have to wash the sweat away and the blood keeps
coming back. I told Nana that if the bush sees her standing there
it won't come for the child. The bush wants to take back the child
so I must not hold her for she can only go through me. She's safe
with James and Nana. I must not even look at her for there are
problems with my eyes. If I have her picture in them, when I
look at the bush they will see her through me and her face will
change to blood and she will run out to the bush and I can't stop
her. I know this because I looked at her once and the door blew
open and I heard her cry and when I looked back at the bush it
had come closer I must not cease my watch.

James just grows older. He does not understand. He does not know
the danger of the bush like I do. I tried to give him the machete
and show him what to cut outside and he took some men to help

him do it but the child just cried, no, screamed, and I knew it had to be the mind that stopped the bush. If James and the men chopped it back, death would come so I must stay here by the window and keep it out by being stronger in my mind. James thinks I've lost my mind but with all this work to do I cannot reassure him. He tries to bring the child to me and can't understand why I scream at him to take her away and give her back to Nana. Nana knows things James and I don't know and the bush doesn't want her, only the child, so she's the safest person in the house. She washes out my muslin dresses and I see them hanging on the line. The bushes think it's me and they bend in the wind to tear them, but Nana hangs them high. Before I put a dress on I search it, in case the wind has blown seeds from the bushes to tangle in the skirts and reach me on the inside. It happened once and when I sat, it scratched me and brought blood and there must be no more blood for all the blood is Gobi's blood and I cannot pay it back and James says pray to Jesus but I can only see Gobi's head shattering and the blood upon the bushes. That's why the bushes want me and the child, for we came with Gobi's blood upon us and I don't know if Jesus cares, for Charles was never ever tried. He just sold up and went away, back across the waters where the bushes cannot find him, but, for the child, James and I must stay.

I am caught between black and white. The child is olive with green eyes. I saw her today. I asked for a mirror and put it between me and the window and asked Nana to stand the child behind me. Maybe if I do not look at her directly she will be safe. She did not cry so I think this was a good idea. I won't do it very often because the bushes might find a way to break the mirror and that will be more bad luck when we have enough already. I think every year on her birthday I will use the mirror but what if when she gets older she won't stand there quietly for me to see. I will have to wait and see and I know Nana will help me for she understands.

James wants to bring a doctor but Nana says to let me be for only time can cure these things. He does not agree, but he has grown so weak and spends all his time in prayer. He is happy to leave these things to Nana and now depends on her completely to bring up the child and to take care of me. I know it will never be over. James does not understand that the threat of the bush will never leave us alone. In the hot months they seem to wilt, but the heavy afternoon showers seems to make them sing and I hear them shouting hallelujahs as the wind shakes the water off them and they stare at me again.

Today they wanted their flowers back. Gobi used to pick the flowers off the bush and bring them to me. I can still smell their perfume. When he was alive the bushes loved me and I wore their flowers in my hair while Gobi held me and the bushes made us our hiding place.

I am not paying them back just for myself I am paying for all the white folk, especially I pay for Charles who killed him. We are linked by white blood and Gobi and I stood no chance. The bushes are only doing what they have to do. I understand now what happened to Adam and Eve in the garden. Eve let him in you see and then they had to run out of the garden to get away from the bush. It was the bush chasing them all the time and the Lord was vexed with them because they let the bush take over his garden. They knew too much because they let their bodies join just like I did with Gobi.

James comes every morning and prays beside my chair. As he rises, he strokes my hair and it reminds me of Gobi but I say nothing. The child's hair is tangly. She cries when Nana brushes it and I get frightened when she cries. I watch her when she runs around the garden. Nana says she is safe for the bush already got her hair and they don't want anything more from her. That relieved me so much but I know I still have to watch because they will come for me. James wants to name her. He christened her in church. Nana held her because I would not go and James was silent when he was to call her name so Nana whispered Susu and now I hear them call her and I like the sound. James came and said he registered her in our surname, Edwards, and that she will be ready for school soon. When she gets a little older he wants to send her to the church school in town where she can get an English education. They will accept her there because I am white and James is known to them. He has bought her a pony and is teaching her to ride. She will have to ride to school in town.

I moved from the chair today. Nana insisted that I try so I walked around the house and looked out the back door and got frightened. The bush has taken over so much of the back garden. With Gobi gone, the work was too much for Nana and James. Then I heard her cry and she came running in with blood on her leg. She has only had a little scrape. Nana tries to reassure me, but I rushed back to my chair. Someone has taken the machete, I can't find it anywhere.

I am screaming. James is shaking me. Nana is hugging the child. Nothing reassures me. I want the machete back so he gives it to me and drags me out of the house into the garden and to the bush I have been watching. 'Chop it, chop it.' I'm chopping away and the bush is tearing back at me. My hands are bleeding but I am chopping and James is screaming at me to chop it all till I can chop no more. I fall to the ground calling Gobi. James pulls me back in the house where he tells Nana to bathe me while he takes hold of the child. All the time in the bath, I hear him singing to her and I know I can't fight the bush. I must make peace with the bush. I dress in clean white muslin and return to my window-seat. I say nothing to them but I smile. The child is sleeping in James's arms. I will be her protecting angel though I can't be a mother to her. Nana will be her real mother and I will be a wife to the bush. That's all that the bush has been asking, is that I submit myself and be still.

FIGURE TWO

I am born of blood. I am born of bush.

Nana told me the story of my father to help me understand my mother. I know why she sits in the corner and stares through a closed-up window, leaving me to grow up without her.

I know why the children sing at the gate and laugh when I throw stones to hit them. They mock and they cry, 'Oh Lord, don't let me be like Emmeline, just sitting by the window and wasting time.'

I am happy when it rains because the children run home and I don't have to fight this war against them.

Yesterday I found a stone that felt like a bird in my hand. It crashed into the head of the last child to run. I know she won't come back tomorrow.

I learnt how to pick mangoes with Nana, how to aim and throw straight, at the stem, not the fruit, so they wouldn't suffer a bruising, and now I know if the children come back, I shall stone them down like ripe mangoes.

Typhoid took them, took them all. It moved through the village like the hand of God. Nana alone was my rock and my harbour as I watched the strange woman sitting in the window waste away till her bones stretched her skin, finally going yellow and giving in. James would not listen to Nana and stay in. He kept on visiting the sick all around till he fell to the fever and we lay them both in the ground. Nana cared for all those who lay around and kept me alive with her bush baths and her teas. I lost all my hair, that long and tangly mass, and I lay bald and thinly white as she kept the hand of death off.

That's when I stopped riding to school in town and though Nana tried to get me to go back, I threw a tantrum every time. I would never return. I would never go back to the teasing of the girls who had threatened to shave me and relieve me of that hair. They felt themselves so pure with their pasty skin and long straight hair. Just being among them was enough to show the world that I was touched by the colour they disdained. I would not go back among them to study their history or learn their English manners or drink their cups of tea.

It took two years for my hair to return, black, long and thick, and waving with curls. Nana spent long hours washing, oiling and braiding it. It was my pride and joy and every time I brushed it out I would parade for her round the living-room and she'd look towards the empty window-seat and sigh. This second growth reminds her of my mother. The tangle of bush had disappeared.

Nana has moved from her cottage to my house. Yes, I suddenly realised it was my house, and we rent out her cottage to Will, the carpenter. Will's son is sixteen just like me and already a trained craftsman. Together we work the vegetable patch at the back of the yard while Nana sees to the house. He calls me Susu instead of Susan and I in return call him Son Son.

There is a special feeling between us in the bush. I weed with strong hands while he's digging. I carry the seeds in my pocket to plant and he sings work songs like we're dancing.

I am a natural dancer. It's not the strict figures we were learning in that school but the dip and sway of the villagers. The bends and turns that the drums added to the quadrille moved my hips in circles and Nana told me how my mother only learnt the first figure and now I was dancing the second.

I had chosen Son Son as my partner and what did he do but go and break his leg running down the path to the river, believing he could fly. I would trust no one else. Son Son and his father Will were new to the village and were not a part of those who had shamed me or sang and laughed at my mother, so I dropped out of the quadrille and spent time reading the very books I had ignored in school.

What's the point of school, I thought. All I wanted to do was marry and have children. I already had land and my own house, more land than most in the village. So I told Son Son in my usual forceful way that I had chosen him to fulfil that role. I thought he would be delighted but he seemed almost scared of me even as he was nodding. I thought then that maybe he was too young and I should look for someone older but I most certainly did not want a man old enough to rule me so Son Son would have to do. Also there was the question of colour. Though he was pale-skinned, almost white, his hair was also thick and curly. I was not having that thin and tangly mass on any of my children. It would make them seem like weak-livered whites rather than strong-blooded children. Also, they would not come out with black skin, but more olive and belonging to sun.

I want children, lots of children and Son Son seems healthy enough and I won't waste time sending them to school. Little good school has done to anyone I know. Son Son would teach the boys carpentry and, well, the girls would marry near-whites. Lots of these illegitimate sons were now becoming overseers on their fathers' plantations or being educated and trained in profession. If only my father had had such luck, but I was determined my daughters would make up for what happened to my mother. I will pick the men carefully and give each girl some land on which Son Son will build each one a house. That will give them their independence. All that was left now was to have them.

I decided to have the first one before marrying Son Son just in case he wasn't capable of fathering children. I will take no chances on my plans. Nana, grown old now, was upset at what she called my fornication, crying all over my mother's grave and appealing to James's spirit, but there was a steel in me that was unmoved. I had always done what I felt right doing. And so the first one came along and her name was Emma, after my mother.

Nana put her all into the wedding. She wouldn't hear of any local celebrations and insisted in getting a vicar from town. From my mother's white muslin she made the most exquisite wedding-dress and filled the church with flowers. She killed two of her pigs and the smell of stewed pork filled the yard, but she didn't book a mento band as she felt deep down that dancing hadn't brought any luck to me or my mother. I didn't care either way and though Son Son grumbled about the lack of a party, I already knew how to get round him. He was an animal in bed and if I didn't throw him out each morning to go and work with his father, he would have given me a new child before my body recovered from the first. But that was just what I had married him for, children, and lots of them. Luckily, my body was young and strong and easily coped with a pregnancy each year. The first two boys came next, William, after his father, and Gobi, after mine.

It was then that the problems started. Men, I don't know how I was so wise to them, but when I first saw Eva hanging around the carpentry workshop I knew immediately he was ready to stray. She was one of those fine-boned and delicate girls who had come out more white than black. I could not understand why the men thought those weak looking women beautiful, as if they needed someone to protect. There was I, strong as a horse, living in my father's body, and he was fooling around right there in front of me as if because I had mothered three children I was ready to be put away. But let him have his fun. He was living in my house, on my land and, apart from the shared earnings with his father, he had nothing.

I kept him long enough for two more children, Ida and Tom, but when Eva herself swelled up big and the whole village knew it had to be Son Son's work, I packed all his belongings in two baskets and delivered them to the workshop.

Let there be space for a good man. I already had my eye on one and within a month I had moved in Woody. Woody was almost white but dirt poor and for him I was a fine catch as women of my colour and wealth would not normally have anything to do with a man like him. He was a labourer who hired his strength out weeding and planting other people's fields and he had often worked for me.

Men's bodies had not interested me before, but I had often watched him in the fields and seen his shined-up muscles move through the bush like a dancer with his machete swinging. Working with him one evening, long after the others had gone home, I had come close enough to smell him and the bush had given him a perfume that overtook my senses and for the first time in my life made me scared of the power of a man. Never had I felt so weak and in need of someone's touch. It was not pretend. I really fell over into his arms and when he caught me I was ready to be taken.

The first night with Woody was something every woman should feel, something every woman should feel and then recover from immediately. He filled me completely and covered me in himself like I was dainty and fragile. Me, a big strong woman, crying like a baby when I came and holding on to him wanting more and more, wanting him back inside me as soon as he pulled out and him strong enough to come back almost immediately. Within two months I was pregnant, throwing up all over the place, unable to work. All the children I had with Son Son had come easy, but this child did not settle into my body. It fought me all the way.

The moon hung over the mahoe trees. The night wind trickled through them. The child lay snug in my belly taking up all the space, making breathing a short and difficult thing. The dogs were restless tonight, wailing at the moon. The heat would not move from the room. I pulled myself slowly out of bed and padded into the living-room. I listened to the children breathing at the edge of their bedroom door. A familiar sound was missing and I couldn't work out what it was. I sat in the chair that was my mother's, a seat I had always avoided, yet tonight it seemed the right place to be. The night hugged me and the new child in my womb relaxed for the first time today. I drifted off with the sense of someone stroking my forehead and suddenly awakened in fear. It seemed like all the air had left the room and then I realised, Nana wasn't snoring.

I knew without believing and sat there willing the sound of her deep sleeping to fill the house as it always did these nights when I sat awake. I knew she had grown weaker over the last few months and my break up with Son Son had moved her to tears. She hardly spoke to Woody and the briskness had left her walk. Breathe, Nana, breathe. I need you more than ever now. I am afraid for this new child. I can feel it taking all my strength and I think it will come soon. I depended so much on Nana. She had cut the birth strings of all the others. They had been so easy to carry and almost birthed themselves, flowing out of my womb like the waters bursting. Nana, my real mother, why don't you fill the house tonight with your breathing. I stopped my own breath just in case it was stopping me from hearing. Frozen in the chair, I thought of waking Woody, but he was such a deep sleeper and so angry when disturbed.

I wrapped my gown around me, gathering my strength to stand and walked over to Nana's doorway and slowly entered her room. A lone dog let out a wailing and I laid my hand on her chest. No sound. No movement. This was no dream. Nana had left the land of the living. I lay my head on her chest, the child crumpled up inside me. Frozen there, except for the tears, I wailed louder than the dogs outside. That's where Woody found me.

The morning broke with strange red clouds. The children's eyes were staring. Death had entered in the night. Death had taken their dawning.

The village had lost their mother. Whatever the stories of the past, everyone loved Nana. The house filled that day and kept on filling. The women brought their biggest pots and smoke filled the yard as the cooking started. The men brought bottles of estate rum and the digging of Nana's grave started. I chose her favourite spot under the mango tree at the side of the back garden. She had always sat down there to rest when we had planted provisions there. William and Son Son came and fell a mahoe tree for the coffin.

The child in my belly just wouldn't rest. It seemed intent on coming. The women insisted I stayed in bed as they took care of the house and the children. I listened to the sounds of the wake, nine nights of singing and drumming, and on Sunday, dressed in white, the church filled for Nana's burial.

Losing Nana took all my strength and the child in my belly held on to all that was left. She tore her path out of me about two weeks later, screaming and hungry. She ruled the house from dusk till dawn. There was no sleeping here now and Woody took to staying out and not coming home till morning. I was too weak to tackle him and the house filled with empty bottles. He was drinking rum like water and started arguments at the drop of a hat.

All Amanda wanted was my breasts. She sucked me dry, day and night and would bite my nipples as they emptied, she on one side of the bed and her father drunk on the other.

Woody gave up working. He slept all day and drank at night in the village square with the losers. The harmony I thought had been mine had disappeared with Nana.

The first night he beat me, I lay stunned, unable to find a voice. I had waited up for him and when he crawled in early in the morning, I had dared to criticise. I was sitting in my mother's chair and watched him come in from the verandah. I will never forget the hand he raised, the shock of the blow he struck me, the stink of the rum lingering on his breath or the cold sweat that broke out from me. I fell back into the chair and lay still, unable to believe what had happened, but there was no one to call, his shadow filled the room and the child woke and filled it with screaming.

I never thought a man could so darken my days. All the light went out of my eyes and even the sight of the children playing in the yard did nothing to bring back my joy. Thank God they were old enough for chores. I set them to carrying water and taught them how to weed the back garden. Other children went to school but mine ran wild and lived on the many fruit trees that filled our land. I sold Nana's cottage to William as he was already living there and I know the village laughed at what they thought was my downfall. I had thrown Son Son out and brought in Woody, thinking I had found a good man. Now I was wondering if there was such a thing and how it was possible to get rid of him, but Woody kept kicking down my door, he was not leaving.

24

How are the mighty brought low.

I am used to the beatings now, but I get my own back when he has to come begging for money. There is power in that and I stand between him and the children. He tries to beat them but I will kill him and he knows it.

Deep down I think he is stupid. I watch him while he sleeps off the rum and I think how easy it would be to kill him. I stand over the bed with the kitchen knife and only the thought that my children would be left alone without a mother stops me from sinking it into his heart.

I have started going to church again. Prayer is my only comfort. There is an old vicar who comes up from town once a month and gives communion. I wish I could take it with the others, but the village has branded me a sinner because I am not married to Woody. He couldn't care less abut church and quarrels about his dinner on Sundays because I dress all the children and take them with me so I don't cook till late afternoon. I have learnt how to ignore him and to avoid the worst of his temper. He has stopped asking for any rights in bed. For some men, especially those who still cut cane down on the plantation, rum takes the place of women and they lose their powers very quickly. It would be easier for me if he was with other women as I could probably get rid of him into someone else's arms, but he likes the easy life he's found with me. He has let his body go and I know the rum will kill him eventually, but how quickly I don't know.

God is good. Woody has fallen off the mule. He rode into town and drank all night on the estate with his friends. Two men from the village found him the next morning and brought him home. He is crippled from the waist down. I help him each morning into my mother's chair and now he sits looking through the window like she did. He is a bitter man and now he cannot hit and is helpless, like a child, he has only his voice to raise. I laugh now in his face and watch it go purple with the wish of killing me. There is nothing he can do except knock over the plate of food I bring him, and that is not good for him as I leave him hungry for the rest of the day while I go to work in the fields.

I have put in several crops this year and I have to organise the workers. There are quite a few men in the village who do not want to go back to working cane on the estate and are available for hire. On the work days I do the cooking for them all. I am determined to make money from the land I have been left from

Nana and James. I will never have friends in the village but I can afford to employ them and that is enough. I am careful now what I pray for. I think my prayers were answered in stopping Woody, so now I pray for health and strength for me and for the children. Emma, the eldest, is now able to take care of the house and the other four are old enough to help her. I have taught them how to take care of the vegetables in the back yard and each Saturday I send them to market in town to sell what we have extra. It's difficult moving Woody from bedroom to the chair each day so I have moved my mother's chair and set a day-bed in the corner and that is where he lives now, shrivelling up in bitterness, totally dependent on me. Every Friday evening I put a bottle of rum beside him. That's his only pleasure now and who would I be to deny him that.

Amanda follows my skirt tail. She is five now and is almost as big as the others. She has not one touch of black in her. She could pass anywhere for white. Her hair has grown long and straight and the other children love brushing it. I have decided to send her to school, to the shock of the whole village. I went to market in town this week and bought her several dresses and some shoes. The child is delighted. I thought she would resist, but when I handed her the slate and pencil, she slept with them all weekend and had her hair washed on Sunday without a tear.

Teacher Jones took her under his wing immediately and now she is coming home with books he's lent her and he chats with me after church on Sunday to say how well she is reading. And so she should. She spends all her time curled up in bed with a book and does no housework at all. I know I spoil her, so the others say, but she soon took on different duties. She does all the sums on market day and reads stories to the others. On Sundays she often reads the sermon in church. The sins of the parents obviously did not descend upon the child.

How the village has grown. It is divided into three parts now, all of them meeting in the village square. There is Friendship, Endeavour and James Gully. When you arrive in the square on the dirt road from town a track which turns left takes you to Friendship. If you go straight through the square you come into Endeavour or you can turn right down into a deep dark valley which is James Gully. All of it together is called Hillside.

The land I have inherited is mainly in Friendship, practically all of Friendship. Not all of it is good for crops as it runs quite steeply down to the gully and to the river called Wise. James and Gobi had realised this and had planted it through with fruit trees.

The rest of it I used for yams and bank crops like red peas and gungo peas. The church is just on the corner of Friendship where it meets the square and a new school has been built in Endeavour which saves the church from doubling as the school.

The village has done all this for itself by holding workdays when the whole village came along to do the work. The wood came from the trees we cut down and William had come from town to supervise the building. That was how he and Son Son had come to live in Hillside.

Our house sits on the flat that tops the hill at the centre of Friendship and from the yard you can see down the hill to the river and across the western mountains. Nana's cottage, which we had sold to William, lies further down the side of the hill, and if you follow the track down to the river, there are several more spots flat enough for building. These, I will give to the children.

In the square, round the corner from the church, is the shop run by Sister Mary and, across the road from her, a rum bar run by Fred.

From the village square, if you look right, you see all the way to the sea and into the town of Lucea on the north-west coast. If you look left you can see down to the plains of Savanna. Hillside is built on this watershed and is full of springs where most of the rivers of the west have their beginnings. It is from these springs that we get fresh water and to grow as a child here is to always be carrying buckets of water from these springs. The rest of our water comes directly from rainfall which we collect by building gutters on the roof and filling up old oil-drums.

Most people who live here own their own plot of land. You can see their relationship to the landowners written in their faces. Because of that it is a strange village as most of the others around are populated by black Africans who have saved and bought their land since freedom. The nickname for Hillside is Mulatto Town and when we go to market in Lucea we are the only near whites selling provisions. Town mulattos are different from us. They are educated and dress in the latest fashions. We are peasants from the hills, no different from the black ones.

The land in Hillside is rich and in order to save it being washed away in the heavy summer rains, most people have planted fruit trees. Because of this the village is rich with crops all though the harvest season. Some of the farmers plant cane which they sell to the nearest mill. It is still the best way to make money. Since the slaves have been freed, the plantations are finding it hard to get labour and though they have brought in Indians and Chinese, they are still struggling for workers. Only the poorest of Africans go back to work on the plantations. It is too much a memory of slavery and the pay is too little for the extra hard work. The luckiest of us have our own plot of land from which we can sell our provisions.

After giving the land for the church and selling Nana's cottage to William, I have six acres left to share between the children. This is a lot of land in a small village where most people own a quarter acre. I have two acres under cane where the land is flat by the river. This is the reason I bought the mule as the freshly cut cane has to be brought to the square to be taken to the factory. I own one of the two mules in Hillside so I also make money hiring it out carry other peoples' crops. Three acres are under bananas, which I know is going to be successful, although it is a fairly new crop for the area. There are banana boats coming to pick up in Lucea harbour. The other acre surrounds the house and it is here I carry on what James and Nana started, growing provisions for the house and taking the extra to market. On this piece of land I still have yams, red peas, sweet potatoes, tomatoes, okras, pineapples, callallo, all kinds of crops to keep a kitchen happy and to sell.

All in all, life here is good. The children are well fed and have a future. Amanda is my last. My childbearing years are over.

FIGURE THREE

It was in this village that I, Amanda Magdalene Wood, grew up. I was poorly from the start and aware from then of the village gossip that my great-grandfather, the plantation owner, was also my grandfather on Woody, my father's side. I worked this out to mean that Woody had the same father as Gobi through a woman slave that he had taken after Nana, and that my mother had committed a sin by taking Woody in. My mother, Susu, however, was a very stubborn woman who believed in herself and said that Nana would have told her and that the whole village was lying. Anyhow, that was the reason everyone held for why I was poorly from the start. Woody, when I asked him said, 'cousin and cousin boil good soup', and didn't seem too bothered. Moreover, he suggested, most people in the village would find similar stories if they looked at their own history.

Always sick, I couldn't work with the others in the fields and Susu decided, against all her beliefs, that I should go to the village school. I loved school. Teacher Jones was a wizard and introduced me to the world of books which became the love of my life, books and books and more books. By the time I was nine, Teacher Jones split the junior class in half and I took them in reading lessons.

My father, Woody, helped a lot. He was such a lonely man. The whole family ignored him. My mother fed him, that was all. So, in the evenings, after school, I started reading to him from whichever books he chose and I could tell he waited for me to come home so I could sit with him in the corner by the window and bring him stories from all over the world. When it got dark, we lit the oil-lamp on his table and I breathed in the smoke as I crouched nearer to it so I could see the words. Most of all, he preferred the readings from the Bible. He was never tired of the Psalms and the Song of Solomon. These were new territory to me and I began to think about love and I wondered how, in a world of such great loves, like Solomon and Sheba, could my mother and my father live without it in their lives. Without any great passion they seem to have settled into their own routine of which I was the only bond left. The only time my mother smiles is when I sit in the corner reading to him. Somehow this gives me hope, because I want a great love in my life. I want to meet my Solomon.

My father is a dreamer while my mother is really practical. She keeps our lives moving and puts food on the table. He probably loved her for her strength but found himself too weak to live with it. It all seemed the wrong way round from the books that I was reading where the woman was the dreamer and the man does all the work.

Friday evenings are the best when she brings him a flask of rum. He lets me pour it for him and once I tasted some. He just watched me as my face crumpled with the strength of it and burst out laughing as I spat. I had never heard him laugh out loud. A rueful smile had always been the most, and always out of sight of my mother. Now, every Friday, he gives me a sip. To teach me to respect it, he says, so that I can't be taken advantage of with drink. When he said that, I became a tragic heroine, going to wreck by drink, over the love of a man. I played all the different parts in the stories I read my father. I wanted to make him laugh more and soon he did. When I played Sheba, he said to me that Sheba was black, not almost white like you, and I felt really hurt that he did not think I could be the greatest queen in love.

I thought the black girls in my school were beautiful. Their skin and hair were shined up with oil and one girl in particular had a face like carved ebony in which sat hazel eyes, the only sign of white blood in her ancestry. Around her, I felt drab and colourless. While their skin shone in the sun, mine went red with brown spots like a mango in its ripening. I suppose there must be something to say for mangoes because, to my surprise, I received more attention from the boys, and I really thought them stupid in their choice.

The other thing I did with my father was sing. He knew all the songs, from slavery days all the way up to the new mento tunes, and, boy, could he sing. I could see how much his body wanted to dance and it was at those moments that I saw what he had lost and I felt most sorry for him. I learnt the songs singing along with him and kept the rhythm by beating a spoon against his bottle of rum.

My mother seemed to hate any kind of music and never went out to the mento yard on a Friday or Saturday night when the quadrille was danced. I decided that as soon as I was old enough, I would dance the nights away. That's if I didn't become a Christian as Teacher Jones said I should and treat such music as sin. My father said Teacher Jones was an idiot and that reading too much without some rum and dancing would make any man a fool. He also said that the time I spent keeping rhythm with him was saving him from madness. Who will you believe, he would ask, your father or Teacher Jones. Life needs a balance of all things, he said, and none should fight against the other for the good Lord placed it all around to share the time of our lives. Teacher Jones quotes the Bible, but without Woody, I would never have found its poetry, just the prophecy of fire and brimstone from the Old Testament that Teacher preferred.

I once asked my mother about forgiveness and she said an eye for an eye and a tooth for a tooth was the only fair way to live, but Woody said the most that turning the other cheek would do is give you an extra slap. My mother thinks he brainwashes me, she says never to trust a man and only choose one you can rule. Like you rule Woody was what I said to her, stopping her in her tracks, so we never had that conversation again. She says I am silently impertinent because when she tries to stop me doing anything I just look straight back at her and say nothing. Then I go ahead and do it anyway and, as I'm poorly, she can't beat me. I had never seen my mother hit a child, so I knew what I could get away with, but I never knew the reason why until one of my sisters blurted it out to me.

I was having an argument with my mother one evening, screaming at her that she didn't care for my father, and Emma slapped me when we went to bed that night and told me all about them. She was seventeen and I was ten when she told me the story of Woody beating my mother. I hated them all then, they had broken the one love I held. They had made my father into a monster. How could I read to him again or sings those songs with him. I would never see him again as an example of the man I would love.

I still read to him now but the laughter has gone out of me. He knows I have changed towards him but he will not tell his own side. Why did they have to let me know, I was all he had and they've broken it. Now I feel I have to choose between him and my mother and that is hard, but more and more I feel that he has paid already for whatever he has done, and I am glad that I did not stop reading to him.

I am fifteen now and Emma's gone. She's married a young man called Edward and her father Son Son has built them a house on the acre of land my mother gave them. My mother used the occasion to tell us how she had divided the rest of the land and now I know this house is mine and the acre of land it is built on. I have already decided that, however long he lives, I will look after my father. My mother, Susu, seems so strong, I don't think she will need me.

I still fall ill quite often. Anything that passes through the village seems to get to me first, from the slightest cold to the longest fever. I had started helping Teacher Jones in the lower classes of the village school, but I'm away ill so often that he couldn't give me a full-time post and had to take on someone new. That was the main reason that I learnt how to sew. I seem to have a natural talent for it so I spent the last year at Miss Harrington's in town, learning how to cut and stitch. Now I have an old sewing-machine set up in the corner by my father, and we talk while I sew. We talk a lot about the women whose dresses I am sewing and sometimes he forgets he is my father and tells me of the ones who were his lovers. Apparently he was popular and wild. He is an unholy man, but what a sense of humour. Somehow, my mother didn't discover that about him. I think I get the best of what's left of him.

I am sewing for a wedding and what fun it's been. Sewing has made me popular with all the women in the village, especially the ones of my generation. I started going to market with my mother and while she sells, I walk around the town and look at the latest fashions. Then I adapt them for the women in the village. I also have a good look at the men for I have not given up looking for my Solomon. The wedding is next Saturday and the maids of honour are here all the time for their final fitting. One of them is from the German village across the mountains from us. She is the sister of the groom's best man. I had always heard of this village where a lot of Germans had come to live as peasants in the mountains. I asked Woody about it and he said the government was bringing them in so there would be no land in the hills for the slaves. I am not sure about this but when I go to market, I see them with their crops and I am fascinated by their blond hair and blue eyes while they ride their donkeys loaded with yams, carrying their machetes.

On the last night of the fittings, her brother came to pick her up to take her back across the hills. I was late with the finishing so Susu said they could stay and leave early in the morning. Her name was Anna and she introduced her brother as Max. He looked just like the prince in the story books. Since I am not black enough, maybe my Solomon is him.

They stayed up with me late that night while I finished all the dresses. He sat in the corner of the room, deep in talk with Woody, while I was caught in the woman's world of fashion and of marriage. What would I give now to get rid of all of them and drink some rum with him. Woody seemed to read my mind, because he poured them both a drink and then said I must be tired and offered me a drop of his. This allowed me a moment free to smile at Max and brush past him to and from. I couldn't think of anything clever to say so I knocked back the rum with a cheer. At least my sewing would impress him. The women were already delighted. I am also very good at shirts so I asked what he was wearing. He had nothing special, just his normal Sunday wear, so I suggested that I measure him and make him a shirt for the wedding which was only a week away. He seemed quite shy to accept so I rounded on Woody to convince him, and, almost blushing like a girl, he finally accepted. This meant I would see him again in the week when he would come to collect it and without the company of other women.

I loved his smell. It was the smell of green bush and sweet orange. I stayed as long as I could moving the inch-measure around him. I would make him a formal white shirt from some fabric I had left over and include a bandana cummerbund for his waist that would look so well against his blondness.

We made him and his sister beds on the floor in the same room with Woody, and my mother was surprised when I was up with the dawn, ready to make breakfast for them. I was known never to rise up early but to work late and drink rum with Woody. I think Susu got suspicious then but she was wise and said nothing to me, but Woody laughed out loud and winked at me and was very warm in his goodbye to Max, inviting him to come whenever he was able.

I made him such a shirt, cut to fit his body. I sat late at night by the lamp embroidering the patterns I made on the front, the finest embroidery that I had ever done. Woody laughed and teased me about becoming a fool for a man and suggested that if we had children they would turn out dundus, which was our word for albino, as Max was blue eyed and blond. I blushed at the very suggestion as I had never slept with a man and to be so teased by a father was difficult to overcome.

He came on Friday evening to pick up his sister's dress and the shirt, and when I got him to try it on, you could see that he was pleased. He said he had never worn a shirt so fine and how much did he owe. I found some bravery despite his close up smile and said my payment would be to dance the quadrille at the wedding. That seemed to stop him for a while as he stuttered that he could not dance beyond the very first figure. I laughed and said that I was as bad but we could learn the rest together. With that promise between us, he left, and I started sweating with nerves. I had never danced the quadrille in public.

How Woody laughed at me that night, but I finally got him to sing the songs and beat out the rhythms on his table while he called the positions and the moves for me, but we only got up to the third figure. I thought that would be enough as it would be a long time to dance with one man and one that I hardly knew.

I sat through the church. I sat through the feast and finally the dancing started. I could see him looking round the tables for me and my first instinct was to run, but his eyes locked steadily into mine and I dreaded that bravery at home. As the couples lined up we took our place and I placed my arm through his and we bowed and we curtseyed and we span and turned and the music went on through the evening. I guided him more than he guided me but he found it easy to follow. He was light and nimble on his feet and our bodies moved easily together. Each time we dropped out at the end of the third as I told him I didn't know the other figures. He would bring me a drink and talk quietly with me in the corner till the band started another quadrille.

I was in seventh heaven. My Solomon had arrived and now I could really be Sheba. He walked me home through the quiet of the mahoe trees, the music lingering behind us. The moon hung high over the mountain to the west and the wind stirred the leaves of the bananas. Surrounded by the silver of the night and the smell of my mother's jasmine, I stumbled over a rock and into his arms and before I could recover, he kissed me. That night the leaves of wild tumeric made us a bed and I gave myself for the first time, wild and like a river flowing through rock and the wild ginger round us as a coating.

Woody knew, and I knew he knew. I had not asked Max to come in. Instead I invited him to join me at church on the following Sunday morning. Somehow I thought that would remove any sin and it would be the start of us as a couple. I was hoping Woody would be asleep, but I should really have known better. His voice brushed out from the dark of the room to come and tell him the stories, but tonight I was no more the daughter he knew and I quickly said I was tired and ran to the privacy of my room, glad that I wasn't still sharing. I heard him chuckle behind me in the dark, but what would I say in the morning.

I hung on to my sheets as the sun fiercely sent its heat through my window. It must be nearly midday. I wished then that my mother was a churchgoer and that Woody could leave the house sometimes, but I had to face them. I looked at my dress hanging over the chair and saw the bright red mark on the skirt. How could I get past them to wash away the stains of my mating. I wanted to stay there hidden all day and I finally understood why couples should really have their space before becoming so intimate. But that was not all that I learnt that month as I waited for my period to show and Max had not come to join me in church and his village was beyond my walking. It would be far too embarrassing to go there looking for him, so I took to my bed, ignoring all else, until my mother began interfering.

She had to interfere really, my vomiting filled the house, and every time I came out to empty the bucket, Woody would call out 'wah sweet nanny goat a go run im belly'. My mother, too late, came to my room to do her woman to woman talk. She got me to write to Max and sent the letter herself with a friend. The story came back that Max was already bethrothed to a fellow German girl from his own village. My mother cursed them all, called them inbreeders and God only knew what stopped her from going over there with her machete. She cursed Woody as well saying he must have known and should have protected an innocent daughter. Woody grew silent in his corner and took all the blame that women through history have placed on men, but I knew I was equally to blame. I had given of myself quite freely.

My sewing-machine went cold in the corner. I packed my needles in the drawer. My father drank his rum in silence now and life seemed to go out of the house. I felt like the plant in my mother's garden, the one they call 'shama-lady'. As soon as it was touched, it curled up its leaves and refused, even with the sun, to re-open. How could I have given my trust to someone I barely knew. How could I have fallen in love not knowing what love makes you do He was to have been my Solomon, the greatest love of my life. I had thought on that night he had committed himself that the act was the beginning of our future. I looked at Woody and wondered about men, do they just take whatever they're given. My mother said when you lie down with a man, he can get up and brush off his trousers, but women rise up carrying the weight that they've left in the heat of their coming.

I hated myself more as the months progressed and hid myself from the village. I knew how everyone would talk about Susu's precious daughter. I imagined Teacher Jones's face and the women in the square with their laughter. I wasn't expected to fall from grace and my mother rubbed it in. She shouted over and over that all the books I had read had given me no common sense and that to lie down in bush was worse than the animals that she was keeping. She seemed most upset that I had not brought him home but had been wild in the bushes like the poorest and just like her mother had been mad in that way, she didn't think she would suffer it from her children. By the time we had to start preparing for the child she became her more practical self and, as I refused to go to market with her, she insisted I sew all the clothing.

Something about the sewing-machine must have been therapeutic because I started talking to Woody again and there was some revival in the corner. He sat there and watched me as I sewed and finally told me to be happy. He said it didn't matter how it had come, a child should always be welcome. He sat with the Bible open on his lap calling out names for my choosing. That's when I decided if it was a boy or a girl, the name would be Solomon or Sheba. This delighted Woody no end, he saw it as a sign of my sense of humour and soon we were father and daughter. This time, however, he gave me no rum, he said he wanted the child to be clever. I remembered then how Solomon prayed for wisdom and understanding, but having a child to carry alone made me pray for health and strength. I didn't want God to think I was too demanding.

Being so close to having a child made me more aware of my mother and looking at her one morning as she worked, I suddenly realised she was tired. Having split up the land between her children, there was less for her to make a living from and suddenly we were in danger of being as poor as the others on their small quarter acre of land. She was still working a large food garden, but the cane land had gone to two sons and the others had the bananas. Now there was me adding another mouth to feed and I knew I would have to continue my sewing. Mother's face in the early morning was haggard and swollen with sleep and I felt even more guilty then to have added more to our needs. I realised that going to market each week and carrying the heavy baskets was taking its toll on Susu. The death of our mule nearly stopped her, but she insisted on taking the twelve mile walk with the other men and women in the village. Suddenly, life had no privilege to offer.

The child came suddenly one Sunday night, I was sure that I was dying. Never again, never again, would I let a man touch me. That one moment of pleasure was not worth the pain of pushing a child from my belly. Susu cut the cord and next morning she buried the afterbirth under the tall mango tree. It was a night I would never forget when that child was handed to me. Sheba was white, even whiter than us, she looked German like Max and his family. When Woody saw her he laughed out aloud. There's no hiding of this family tree. Max could not say that it wasn't him.

Woody was sure that he would come to take a look at the child. He explained how men were never sure even if it was their wife they were bedding, and that they would wait till the child was born to be sure it was really their own, and if they did not want to come, they would send their mother or a close relative of the family. I thought that was an easy way out and how many children must have been denied if their looks didn't match up in the family's eyes. No way was Max going to do that to me. I was tearing out his part on her family tree.

My chance came in Sheba's sixth year. By this time I did not mind being seen in public with her. I took her to the village fête that year dressed in a pretty frock I had sewn her. I watched her running around the square with the other children and wondered why I did not find her beautiful like the whole village did. It was then that Mrs Hull rode up. She was the owner of the Great Valley plantation a few miles to the east. Her husband had died the year before and left her with their young son. Sheba, full of courage as usual, went straight up to her horse and started stroking him. Mrs Hull got off and picked her up and put her on the horse to sit. She, the child and the horse seemed delighted with each other and after a good half an hour Mrs Hull turned round and asked who was the mother.

Two weeks later, I packed Sheba's bag, and sent her off to the Hull plantation. Mrs Hull wanted a companion for her son who would not look out of place in the home and Sheba was the chosen one.

FIGURE FOUR

I am cold at night. My new mommy says I have to sleep with the windows open because growing children need lots of fresh air. The room is so big that I sometimes wake up and think about the small room that me and my old mommy used to share. I don't like sleeping alone, but that's the only time I am sad because my new home is beautiful and the farm is big with lots of animals to play with. Mommy Hull, that's what I call her, has given me the guinea pigs to look after. My new brother, John, he is ten, loves the dogs. He has three of them. They are big and shaggy and make me a little bit afraid when they come running up and knock me over. John laughs and says girls are not strong like boys and then rolls on the floor in the kitchen with them. The cook is always trying to get them out and I'm sure that's why John loves to run in through the back door with them. At my old house, dogs would never have been allowed in and we chased them if they came near to the kitchen.

Mommy Hull throws lots of parties and now I have so many pretty dresses for them. John and I are allowed to sit at dinner with them and then we watch the dancing for a while before we're sent to bed. I practise all the dances that I see. I try to get John to be my partner but he refuses and says dancing is stupid. I sometimes chat with the band when they are setting up and I've asked for guitar lessons, but Mommy Hull says I must start with the piano. The parties are the best time in the house and I've learnt all the four figures of the quadrille.

On my tenth birthday Mother Hull threw me the most wonderful birthday party and she insisted that John had to partner me for the ballroom dancing. He is fourteen now and hates the lessons he is forced to take. He moves very stiffly and keeps saying he doesn't want a sister, that he never asked for a sister and that a brother would have been much better because then he wouldn't have to dance.

It's not only dancing that I like. John and I have lessons on weekday mornings with our tutor, Mr Jones. He's from Wales and just graduated from a university called Cambridge which he seems very proud of because he speaks about it all the time and says John will be going there. I asked at dinner last night if I could go too but everyone was quiet and Mother Hull said to drink my soup.

Mr Jones said he wanted to see the colonies before he settled down back home. He's a funny man and almost dances with the long stick that he uses to point things out on the board. He tips up on his toes a lot and looks like he's mimicking a ballet dancer. I remember everything he says and everything he writes down because I can see him doing it in my memory and I like his sing song voice. Most of all I like Geography. I love all the maps of the different countries he has pasted on the walls and Mommy Hull has shown me where her family come from. She has named the house after it and I roll it round my tongue. Llandewy. Llandewy. Mr Jones sometimes speaks a little bit of Welsh for us. He says he doesn't know it very well apart from a few phrases, but it reminds my of my sick grand-father that I left behind at home when he used to speak like the people in the village instead of speaking pure English like my old Mom used to do. The servants in the house speak that sing songy language too and I try not to speak like them because I am not a servant and I don't want anyone to think that I am poor so I'm very careful with my English and pay lots of attention in the classes and try to sound like Mother Hull.

I also make sure I do not dance like the servants though I watch them through my window when they are dancing in the yard. The music is so catching that sometimes I feel my body moving against my will, but I control myself and stop my back from bending and my hips from shaking like theirs do. I will dance like the ladies in the great house. I will keep the men at arm's length and only let the music touch my toes.

My birthday party was a great success. I danced the ballroom quadrille with John who held me stiffly, but I did not mind because it helped me keep my back straight. My new dress was so beautiful that I looked like a princess and my long straight hair had been piled into curls on the top of my head. Not even John could spoil it. We were allowed to stay up late and Mother Hull let us have a glass of wine.

John doesn't like it because I'm growing taller than him now I'm in my teens. Mother Hull says I am growing out my dresses much too fast. John's grown thick and broad across the shoulders and he's doing harder lessons than me. Mr Jones says he has to be prepared for entering university. His next birthday will be his eighteenth and I am only fourteen and a special party is being prepared for him. It seems to be more than a party. The house is being turned upside down and cleaned and there's a new overseer for the plantation. I notice Mother Hull is packing a lot of things away in travelling trunks. She says John has to go to England for university and she has to go to settle him in. She is crying as she says these things to me and I know something is very wrong because she has put an empty trunk in my room and the servants are packing my clothes in it. Suddenly I think, she's taking me to England and I rush into her room and tell her how much I will love going there with her but she is silent. She doesn't say a word.

The day after John's party, an old dirty buggy pulls up in the yard. The woman in it looks at me and that look cuts across the years and I remember something of her but not all. Mother Hull has my trunk put in the buggy and asks me if I remember my mother and says it's time for me to go back home.

I am stricken. Where is home? Llandewy is my home. I must go to England with my family. What does she mean that I must go back home?

The woman by the buggy is looking at the ground. Mother Hull says she is my mother and asks me if I don't remember her. I am set adrift. Suddenly life is over and the mother I have lived with and have loved for all these years, the family I thought was mine, has become cut off in a single moment and I am lost, lost. Mother Hull becomes the traitor of my life and John doesn't even care enough to say goodbye. Mother Hull is crying, but that is not enough. Why won't this other woman look at me instead of standing like a servant by the buggy? The servants are all at the windows watching. I must not break down and scream. Ladies do not do that. I hold my back straight and climb into the buggy. The woman joins me and we ride away.

The house is dark and dingy and smells old. The day bed by the window is empty and I have vague memories of an old man lying there. This new mother says he was my grandfather, Woody, and he has passed away. She takes me into one of the two dark bedrooms and says the old woman lying on the bed is my grandmother, Susu. The skeleton on the bed reaches out a bony hand towards me. I do not want to touch her but I do because I notice she is crying and I think I feel the same way too.

40

My mother and I will have to share the other room and that is an added embarrassment. I am used to my own room. I am fourteen now and my body needs its privacy from everyone, especially from this mother who told me, on the journey here, that she had given me away for my own good and had not expected me to come back home. I can see that she is angry too. Together we drag the trunk into the bedroom. She opens it gingerly and runs her hands over the beautiful fabrics. She tells me there'll be nowhere here to wear them except maybe to church on Sundays and even there they'll cause a stir. She pulls out a drawer full of cotton and immediately starts measuring me. She says she will make me some simple dresses for the kind of work I'll have to do. There'll be housework and there'll be field work, she now tells me, to make up what she earns from the sewing-machine. I know my schooldays are all over, but I place the books I've brought on the window ledge beside the day-bed. For a moment this mother looks at me strangely as if I've stirred up memories she can't abide or as if I remind her of some-one else. She does not speak except to say that there'll be little time for reading as it is now planting time and the little piece of land that we have left will need to be dug up and be filled with next year's seeds. I stare at her as if she were a stranger. I have no intention of ruining my hands. Maybe if there were animals to care for, I would have some idea of what I had to do, so I told her that where I was coming from only black people were sent out to work the land. She looked at me and burst out laughing and asked me just where I was thinking I came from. It doesn't matter how little black blood you have, you will have to work the land. I ask her for the toilet and she says that the latrine is outside the house and round the back. It takes me two days to be so desperate as to use it and when she brings me a wad of rough brown paper she says I'm a little lady who doesn't know life.

The kitchen is out on the other side of the house with a shed for wood beside it. She hands me a small machete and says to cut some wood for the fire. I nearly losen a finger with the first chop and she takes it away and teaches me how to use it and how to catch a fire. Choking from the smoke, I walk away from her back to the house and curl up on the daybed with a book. She will soon learn that she sent me away to become a lady and a lady was what she'd got.

She seemed to accept this and next morning said I'd have to do the housework. I must admit I was sorry for her so I decided to give that a try. The worst task I have is to empty Susu's bedpan in the morning, but I stop my breath and do it. I am so scared of that room where the old woman is dying and I don't want to be there when it happens. She reaches her hand out to touch me all the time but now, as her hand gets weaker, I get more scared and I wish that Mother Hull would come and get me and tell me it was an awful mistake.

I can't hide my crying at nights from my mother and she gets really angry and says that I have a good life even if it's not a rich one, but I hate it, I hate it here. There is a smell in the house that I associate with dying and that's just what happened, my greatest fear. I went in one morning to remove the bedpan and I just knew she was dead, the way she was lying with no sound of that loud breathing and no attempt to touch my hand. I ran screaming out of the room. My mother was in the kitchen making the fire for breakfast and she came running into the house. I couldn't stop screaming and ran straight to my bed, pulling the sheets around my head. I stayed there all day feeling cold and alone. My mother did not come near me. I could hear the house fill with neighbours as the news passed around. Susu was gone but all I could think of was her hand reaching out to touch me, that old, wrinkled, bony hand, reaching out to touch me. I wanted to run all the way back to Great Valley but there was no one at home in Llandewy and I couldn't run to England to find them, but one day I would, yes, one day I would, one day I would run all the way to England.

I will not go to the funeral. The house is full of noise all week. My mother has bought a lot of rum and her father's friends have filled the house with their singing. Out in the yard under the big mango tree they play a game passing rocks around and the others are digging a new grave beside Woody's. That's the part of the yard that I'm most afraid of. All the family are buried there and, although I didn't know them, I keep feeling them all round me. The graves are on the far side of the latrine which makes going there at night really frightening. I watch through my bedroom window as they dig and pass round the rum. When I die, I don't want to be buried here. I want to go to the churchyard. I'm going to go to church every Sunday because I'm scared of dying. Suddenly I realise, it's just me and my mother left. What will I do if she dies. I find myself praying all the time, praying for my mother, that she may live a long life. I must help her with the work. I mustn't let her tire herself out. I never thought of death before but now my mind is full of it all the time. I lock my window tight at night even when it's hot and I am sweating.

Mother has moved into Susu's room and now I really miss her. Sleeping alone with the graves outside makes me think of ghosts and I cover my head with the sheets so I can't see all the leaves moving.

Life and death are too close in this house. I am eighteen now and my mother has chosen to celebrate by opening a large trunk in her room where she has stored what she calls her special clothes. She says I am a woman now and she is growing old and I need to take on some responsibility. She shakes out a dress, an embroidered scarf and underwear and says she wants to be buried in them beside her mother. She only frightens me more. I must get my mind off the dying.

The village is having a dance tonight. The mento band is playing and everyone will be dancing. My mother warns me about the men and says not to let them walk me home because night, and the full moon, and the scent of bush, do something strange to women. I ask her how she knows and she says who feels it knows it. Then she tells me about my father and what he did to her and I begin to understand her story.

I turned out to be the queen of the dance. I held my back straight and kept my hips quiet, and watched the other girls who dipped and swayed and looked like a bunch of loose women. Any gentleman there would know the difference, but by far the best dancer was Curry. The band played the first four figures as I knew them but struck up on the fifth, a wilder music that I did not know. Curry asked me to dance to that tune but I refused and said it wasn't for ladies. I was delighted that he took a break too and brought me some punch which was cooling. He explained why they didn't dance the ballroom way and it was obvious that he knew the difference, with the four couples on the points of the square and only two moving at one time together. He said when you worked hard all the time and just had one night to dance, it seemed silly to stand still and wait or just dance four figures when you could add more. He said he would teach me, but I politely refused. I watched how they stood in two lines, not a square, and showed off as they added new moves.

I remembered what my mother said and slipped away and walked home alone, but desire had woken up in me and when Curry came to the house one week later and introduced himself to my mother, I was ready to dance with him more.

Mother said to make sure he married me first before I decided to lie down beside him. And whatever you do, stay away from the bush, remember you have your own bedroom. Dancing the quadrille week after week built up so much tension inside me and Curry started visiting on Saturdays when he knew my Mom was at market.

I have managed to hold him off all of this time but it's beginning to get more difficult. He says he's a man and he's got needs and I am the woman he wants. I say to him what about marriage, but he says that will come later.

My mother keeps on warning me about men and she says she has heard at the market that Curry has gotten another woman pregnant, a young Indian girl from a peasant family who just moved into the village. I asked him about it but he said the child wasn't his, and I don't know who to believe. He is getting more and more persuasive and finally one Saturday I give in to him and now our Saturdays are regular. I keep telling myself, he can't be lying to me, and if I have his child, he will marry me. It's not long before I tell him, in delight, that I'm pregnant.

I have never seen anyone grow so cold so quickly. I suddenly remember Mother Hull, putting me into the buggy, a terrible feeling of imminent departure and the end of what I had grown used to. I am right about this feeling because Curry has stopped coming to the village dance and has ended his Saturday visits. I can't hide my morning sickness from my mother and she says to me, bitterly, that she had warned me about men but I just did not listen. She says that the big talk at market is that the father of the Indian girl has beaten him up like a dog and insisted he take care of his daughter. He has marched them into church for a wedding. My mother's eyes are dark with her own memories and I realise I don't have a father to beat up a man for me. So here I am, expecting a child, for a man who is now married into a nearby family. We cannot help but meet each other and sometimes, at the shop, I see Vera, his wife, her belly only slightly bigger than my own. Suddenly Curry is not the gentleman I thought him to be and I retire from the dance to look after my new baby. He hangs his head low when we see each other in the square, but twice now he's met my mother at market in town after selling his stock. He has given her money for me. He says he will continue supporting his child even though he has married another and for this reason, he's gone up in my mother's esteem. She has talked him into coming round to see the child, a little girl who I named Sarah. She is a bouncing white baby with his black and straight hair and my mother says she resembles the Germans.

I wish I had listened to my mother for my youth is over and our funds are low and I miss the dancing on Fridays. This is until I weaned little Sarah and once she stopped breastfeeding I leave her with my mother and start going to the dance again. I'm determined not to live alone like she did. There are other men out there in the world and I am going to marry one of them.

My offer came from the least expected source. I had never really looked at black men. Only a few lived around Hillside, but recently more had moved in. As I drank and smoked and danced in the night, playing the village queen, I simply looked for the best dancer in the crowd. One man stood out, his straight back and slim hips, he made the beat seem his own. Black Fred, they called him – there was a white one – became my partner in the dance. Together we danced in the ballroom style. I never thought anyone could dance like Curry or behave like he was from the great house. Black Fred turned out to be a perfect gentleman and it wasn't so strange being with him for a few of the Hillside women had now married with full African men. Fred rented land from nearby planters and was a hardworking man. Each week he brought me a basket of fruit and vegetables. He always brought a special fruit for Sarah and she had grown very fond of him so when he asked me to marry, I was already quite fond of him. He went and spoke to my mother, who was already the sole bread winner, and told her she would not have to worry about me and the child, he would take care of all of us.

My mother made my wedding dress. Black Fred looked tall and elegant in his church suit. This is the closest I came to my dream. The dream I had of going to England and marrying a real Englishman. Not the Hillside white men with their unseen touches of black who lived as poor as, sometimes poorer than, real blacks, so I walked up the altar with Fred, sure that he would stay by my side and wondering what our children would be like. But as the years passed and no children came, Sarah was my only child.

TAKE ME TO THE BRIDGE

Sarah grew fast
Sarah grew tall
Sarah worked hard in the fields
Sarah did not sing
Sarah did not dance
But Sarah was bright in school
Sarah was the first
To pass her exams
Sarah got a job
As a teacher
Sarah took no man
Sarah had a plan
Sarah wanted to get out of Hillside

THE FIFTH FIGURE

Come, come, chile
Let we sing the song again
This time we going to dance
We going to dance through sun and rain
We going to dance until we laughter
Wear out all the pain
We going to laugh till all the neighbours
Think we gone insane
Come, come, chile
Let we sing the song again

She gone
Mi madda gone
She gone to nursing school in Kingston
And she leave me with mi granny
In the wooden house in Hillside
An mi granny teach me all the songs
She singing
Come, come, chile
Let we sing the song again
For yuh madda gone to Kingston
And that is far away
No need to run and follow
Yuh granny here at home
She will take care of yuh
So let we sing the song again
Yuh fadda is a black man
He don't born out of our race
He come from down the flat land
And he have big education
For his father was a preacher
Down there on the plain
So run come chile
Let we sing the song again
Yuh father come to visit
To visit our little village
He steal yuh mother heart
And send her home with child
That's why yuh hair so rough girl
That's why yuh skin so dark

All the rest of we in Hillside white
And turn red in the sun
But you not like yuh madda
Yuh get yuh fadda skin
An yuh brown, brown in the sunshine
And it don't wash off in the rain
So run come, chile,
Let we sing the song again
Run, come, chile
Granny will wash away the pain
You don't belong to our tribe
But we will keep yuh till she come
And we will let yuh father visit
Though he black and his lips red
Like him come over here from Guinea
He black like Pappa Fred
But he support you since yuh born
And he seem to love yuh madda
Yes, he take care of yuh, chile
He behave like a good fadda

So sit still now with Granny
She will try to comb yuh hair
Though it rough and tangle easy
Don't cry when she use the comb
Sing girl, sing chile,
Or the comb will break in two
If yuh pull away the plaits
While we combing it for you
Four long plaits we making
Hanging down yuh back
Thick, thick plaits of rough black hair
And the oil to shine it right
The oil to make it comb easy
Look how yuh pretty when yuh smile

Your father coming up today
In that little car he drive
And he will bring you a present
He will be here in a little while

Is true, mi granny tell me
Daddy bring me a baby doll

One week before mi birthday
And the doll have one big smile
And when yuh squeeze, she wee wee
And yuh have to change her panty
So Granny Sheba teach me to sew
She take little scraps of cloth
That everywhere around the house
And she cut them in triangles
And show mi how to stitch them
Into nappies for the doll
And I so little and clumsy
I stick mi finger with the needle
And Granny laugh
And say to suck it now
And that will stop the bleeding
And she ease mi with a story
And she calm mi with a song
Saying
Come, come chile
Let we sing the song again
Come, come chile
Whether in sunshine or in rain

Smile now chile, for your father is here
Smile now chile, don't you shed no tear
Look how yuh daddy glad to see yuh
And yuh look just like him
And yuh have the same birthmark
Underneath yuh chin

One day me and mi cousins
Go into mi madda drawer
And we take out all her lipstick
And all her face powder
We pretty up we faces
Bright red lip and pink on cheek
We pull out all her high heel shoes
From under the wardrobe
We put on her pretty church hat
And her shawl aroud we waist
That's when Granny Sheba call mi
And say that mi father come
I trying so hard to wipe mi face

I trying so hard to loose the lace
To unfasten the buckle on the shoes
And still Granny Sheba shouting the news
Come now, chile
Your father is here
Ah hope yuh not making
A mess in there
But where is that dratted child I'm calling
She soon come father
She not hard of hearing
And ah run out the door
With mi frock wrong side
And lipstick plaster all over mi face
When ah reach out and see him there
I am speechless as usual
When mi father appear
Talk up now, chile, Granny Sheba say
Come greet yuh father in a special way
Give him a smile
Give him a kiss
It's your father, chile
Though it's your mother you miss

Mommy will soon come home
Soon come home
Mommy will soon come home from Kingston
In the meantime, here's yuh father
Don't behave like yuh afraid of him
Though he fierce and proud
And black of skin
Though he threaten yuh sometime
With belt and stick
We know he don't want yuh to talk like we
We know he want you to speak English
We know he don't want you to poor like we
For he come from a rich black family
So try talk to him jus like the queen
When he come back, chile
Talk like the queen
And try learn to use
Your knife and fork
For yuh father don't want no bush pickney
Yuh father don't want no bush pickney

He want yuh to be a little lady
That's why yuh mother gone away
To study nursing in Kingston
He fill her head with ambition
He don't want yuh mother to be weeding yam
To be weeding yam like Granny
So yuh have to be bright in school my dear
Yuh have to be bright in school
For yuh mother was bright
And yuh father was bright
And is the two of them that bring you

All the little children
Go to the little school
Under a tree with teacher
Where the breeze blow cool
One, two, three and A B C
And nursery rhyme we learning
'Speak the truth and speak it ever
Cost it what it will
He who hides the wrong he does
Does the wrong thing still'

No, Granny Sheba
Ah telling no lie
Is loss I loss the pencil
No, Granny Sheba
Don't make mi cry
Is break I break the slate

I promise I will listen to teacher
I promise I won't be a bother
Soon it will be time to go to big school
I must know my numbers and my letters
Before mommy come home
Before mommy come home
I must know my numbers and my letters

Mommy come home and rent a place
Round the road in Endeavour
It's the first time anyone in the family
Moving our of Friendship
But Hillside small
And it's not far

I can still run back to Granny
Now Mommy qualify as a midwife
And need a place to call her own
She need a place for when Daddy come
A place where he can sleep with her
And when Mommy gone to work
When Mommy gone to work
I skip all the way to Granny
I can hear her voice from over the hill

Run come, chile
Let we sing the song again
Come quick, chile
Let we sing the song again
And I run through the bush
Past the hog plum tree
Daddy say don't run on the road
One day I didn't listen to him
And ah didn't know he was in the rum bar
When he see me
He draw his belt
He draw his belt to warn me
And ah run with mi tears
Ah run with mi tears
All the way round to Granny

Granny Sheba and Papa Fred
The two of them never harm me
And when bush macka juk me
And break inside mi foot
Papa Fred pick it out with a needle
When he come home from bush
Every evening when he coming home
He bring a basket of fruit
He stop in Endeavour and leave it for me
On his way home to Friendship

Ring a ring a roses
I have two new friends now
They live beside me in Endeavour
One name Peter
One name Grace
And we play like Mamma and Papa
Grace and Peter are sister and brother

So I have to play Peter's wife
We build a dolly house
From some bamboo in the bush
And we make a little bed
Of tambric leaves and grass
And Peter and I lie together
We touch one another
In we secret place
And start learning all about pleasure
We play a little game
That teach us where to touch
'Yah so Mr Finnigan
Yah so, sah,
But yah so no sweet
Like yah so sah'

One day rain falling
So we can't go to bush
Me and Peter lock weself in the toilet
I pull off my panty
And he start feel me up
When mi mother come and open the door
When she see what we doing
She scream and she bawl
And drag us all the way through the village
She tell everybody
All along the way
About the rudeness between me and Peter
She take me to Granny Sheba
And repeat the story
And Granny say
No badda vex
No badda beat her
For is a childish game
Is really not a sin
It better you explain it to her
So Mamma tell me about the rudeness
Between a girl and a boy
And say I too young now
To explore it
And she say I must pray
That sin don't come my way
I must pray that the bush don't come and hold me

From that day I frighten
About what lay between my legs
But I can't forget the pleasure that it give me
And I wait until my mother
Gone to work far away
When she gone to deliver another baby
Then I run to the bush
With Peter, without Grace,
Though she cry that we don't want her with we
But soon Grace find a boyfriend
We call him Bunny
And we have a good time playing
Like two different family
And we touchie touchie
Till the bush done sweat we

So my mother get a lady
To stay with me each day
But that turn out worse than you could imagine
Because the lady, she name Fay,
Want me to touch her same place
And she burn mi pon mi han
Using the clothes iron
And say if I don't do it
She will tell a lie on me
And if I tell my mother
She will burn me again
Burn me again with the clothes iron
So I cry and I cry
When my mother leave for work
I say don't leave me here
Don't leave me here with Fay
But mi mother say it good for me
To stay out of the bush
She don't want me to grow up like wild animal

Then I started going to the basic school
And I brighter than the rest of Hillside children
And the teacher say
She expect a lot from me
For mi mother did bright
And mi father did bright
And between them I must have the pedigree

So she preparing me to go to big school early
And by the time I am six
I can read any book she put before me

Now I'm walking two miles
To the big school in Retreat
A bigger village near to where we are living
And I reading so well
The teacher split the class in two
And I reading story to the littler children

By this time, Fay is gone
And I stop playing with Peter
Because I leave for school early
And I reach home after dark
And there's only time to bathe
And do my homework
I wake up before dawn
Put on my uniform
And walk the two mile to the school in Retreat

My father only come up once a week
He live in the seaside town called Lucea
But everytime he come
He take out the dictionary
And test me on my spelling
And I have to give the meaning
He say I must talk to him in English
And I have to stop playing
With the other Hillside children
And settle down to do the work from school
Then he give me the poetry of Omar Khayyam
And a book called *The Prophet* by Khalil Gibran
He talking all the time about Shakespeare
He tell me stories bout the crowning of the queen
He more English than my white grandmother
One day he bring her a big radio
And when I sleep with Granny Sheba
When my mother gone to work
I wake up eight o' clock in the morning
To the sound of the BBC
And the whole house listen to the world news
My father question me when he come

After he order me to bring him
A drink of white rum
He test me on my general knowledge
While we sitting on the verandah
But the evenings when Daddy don't come
Papa Fred will sometimes make a fire
Under the breadfruit tree
And the big people tell different story
I wrap up in my mother skirt
Because I'm frightened of the stories about ghosts
I won't go to bed on my own
When daddy not there
I sleep beside my mother
And I'm always dreaming that she gone
I'm always dreaming that she not coming home
And when I wake up in the night
I hug her up tight
Because I frighten that my mother gone away
I told my dream to Granny Sheba
She always tell me not to worry
That my mother not ever going to leave me
And then she sing the song loud to me again
Come, come, chile
Let we sing the song again
This time, chile
We going to dance through sun and rain
We going to dance until we laughter
Drive away the pain
We going to laugh till all the neighbours
Think we gone insane
And when Granny Sheba
Done sing the song
I wake up in the morning
And make my way back home
My mother tell me she deliver
Another baby in the night
And when she come home in the morning, she very very tired
But she smiling all the same
And that's when I notice
That her belly big again
And she say I'm going to have
A sister or a brother
She smile and she ask me

Which one would I prefer
I say I want a sister
To play with me
I want a little sister
To dress up like me
To push her in the swing
Under the mango tree
I was gone to school when my sister born
When I come home
My father face was a storm
He beat me cause I was late
As I walk through the gate
I crying for my mother
And he say I can't see her
For she just deliver
And she resting with the new baby
So I sit down and cry
Under the mango tree
Because my mother going to love her
More than me
And I vex with my father
For keeping me away
When I go to sleep that night
I remember how to pray
Lord, don't take my mother
Away from me
Lord, please don't take my mother
Away from me
I wake up in the morning
And see the new baby
She have a headful of hair
She look just like me
I tell my mother I will look after she
I going to save all my books
For when she can read
And my mother smile and say
It will be a long time yet
And she say that we will call her Beth

I watch Beth grow
I watch her play
I miss her when I go to school everyday
I bring my sweetie home

Though she too small yet
Then suddenly one day
My mother hug the two a we
And say we moving to a new district
For she get a new job down by the sea
A different village to deliver baby
I ask if Granny Sheba coming too
My mother say, no
And I don't know what I'll do
To be far away from granny
And from Papa Fred
Who am I going to run to
When my father beat me
Who am I going to sleep with
When Mommy deliver baby

A big truck come
And move the bed and chair
And my father drive we
Down to Mosquito Cove
That's the name of the village
Down there on the coast
The new house small and pretty
And I have my own room
But the very first night
I hold on to my mother
And my father get angry again
And say a big girl like me
Should leave room for the baby
And the three of them in the big room
My heart just lock up with gloom
And I want to run back to Granny Sheba
But it's twelve miles away
That's what my father say
He measure it when he was driving
On the road from the hills
I remember it still
The road down to the coast
Where every tree harbour a ghost
I pray every night
To go back to Hillside
But it's a new life that we starting by the sea
A new school called Cove that took me in

Granny Sheba had told me
It was a African free village
All the people black
My mother stand out
It's like she come from England
And not just from nearby Hillside
But soon the people know her
As she walk from house to house
Delivering them baby
And naming some of them
A whole new generation
Passing through her hand
She say she come a long way
From her young days in Hillside
Where the children had called her Hitler
When the war was on
Because she was so white
And had a little German
She had to hide from them
And she always saying
It not good to be white and poor
So she glad to leave the village
And start off on her own
With me and Beth as little children

She was such a good mother
And she made a happy home
But there were terrible days
When Daddy come
He did drink so much
When he come back from the rumbar
He take the belt to us
And I started to learn anger
I long for the day
When I grow up big
To hit him back
Take the belt out of his hand
I glad when he gone home to his wife
And we all alone with we mother
School became the other place of grace
All the stories teacher read
The books would swell my head
But the best of it all was the dancing

One teacher showed us the quadrille
And when I visit Hillside
I show off the steps to Granny Sheba
Who laugh from the bottom of her belly
When I sing and move my hips
She say I dancing it jus like black people
Ah bend mi back and wine mi waist
And singing louder still
Granny call Papa Fred to watch me

I was nine years old when teacher say
I must take the common entrance exam
And I pass to enter the grammar school
It's like the whole universe open up to me
There were teachers from all round the world
And so many subjects
Had my head in a twirl
Books and books galore
Playmates by the score
And a dance class after school
But my father, he did rule
That I have to come home early
There was a four o'clock bus
Another come at five
So I stay and play and dance and jive
I tell a lie when I get home
That I miss the bus by seconds
And had to take the later one
But Daddy would still beat me
I willingly pay the price
So I could stay and dance
And learn folk songs and stories
So I buried all my worries
And in the evenings on those days
When my father did not come to stay
Mommy would take us in her room
And recite many poems to we
I listened to her most carefully
And learnt all of the words
'If' from Rudyard Kipling
and most from writers unknown
My mother had such a lovely voice
She gave them a lot of expression

I learnt the art of poetry
Right there in my mother's bedroom
What a lovely evening it would always be
Beth and me in the bedroom with she
And no father standing over we
Like some violent dictator

I don't know what get into my mother head
Because the grammar school was in Lucea
Which was about twelve miles away
Where Daddy lived with his wife
Mommy said the travelling too much for me
And sometime the bus comes late
So she send we to live with Daddy and his wife
In the town of Lucea
The wife never like we
Daddy still a beat me
And I can't stay for a minute after school
Or he would drive up there to get me
I wanted to stay for dance and sport
But as I get on to the netball court
The little car drive up
Is Daddy come to get me
To avoid the embarrassment
I walk home quick
As soon as the school bell ring
But a group of boys from the common
Now following me all the way
They shout at me
They pull my hair
They throw my books in the bush
One day as I reach the gate
I pick up a stone and fling
Just like I use to fling in Hillside
Fling pon the mango tree
I aimed it right in the midst of the group
I let go the stone with force
And I hear the crack
When it hit one in the head
I hear the scream
I am sure that he is dead
And I run in through the door
Leaving him with his head in blood

The whole group of them run away
And they never trouble me again
They never trouble me again
So each day I walk in peace
To and from school
Not a day did I miss
I wish I was at school all the time
I didn't want to face my father in the evening
When he come in drunk on the rum
I remember, I was barely ten
In the house with him and his wife
When he ask me a question
And I couldn't answer
And he go to the wardrobe for the belt
As he turn around
I grabbed it from him
And looked him straight in the eye
Holding the belt well tight
I saying to him
This is the very last time
This is the very last time, Daddy
This is the last time you going to hit me
I pulled myself up straight
And stared him down
He wasn't footsure
Because he stumbling with the rum
He realised it was the end
I see the weakness of an old man
The weakness of an old man come on him
For he was twenty years older than my mother
And just like a little old man
And I wondering
What I was afraid of for so long
His eye drop away from mine
And I know I win the battle
That the beatings were a crime
And I say
Take me home to my mother
I not staying here one day longer
And I pack the suitcase
With me and Beth clothes
And marched with her out to the car
For some reason I couldn't understand

He bow his head
He take the car key in his hand
And drive we back home to Mosquito Cove
Drive we back home to we mother
When we reach there
I don't say a thing
I just hug her up tight
And Beth just cling
Daddy say that he bring we home
Because I'm silently impertinent
And staring him down
And he don't give a damn anymore
Whether I reach school late
Or even make it through the door
And he disappear to Mr Stanley rum bar
And I wish he wouldn't come back anymore
But he show up in the evening
Stink with rum
And in a while I hear him snore
This year I thankful
When holiday come
And I get to go back to Hillside
Where Granny Sheba still in residence
And Papa Fred so very different
And I pack my belly full
Of all the fruits that he grow
And work with him daily
In the fields down below
And I get to ride the donkey home
Come evening time
Cool evening time
I hear Granny Sheba
Singing out the rhyme
Come, come, chile
Let we sing the song again
Come, come, chile
Let we dance through sun and rain
We going to dance till all we laughter
Ease away the pain
We going to laugh till the whole nation
Think we gone insane
So run come, chile
Let we sing the song again

And suddenly
Like a steep drop off a mountain side
Holidays are over
And it's back to Mosquito Cove
Glad to see mi madda
But fearful of mi fadda
And I find he coming more often
So I wonder about his wife
Why he wouldn't leave my mother
So we could get on with our life
Now every evening after school
Daddy sitting on the verandah
And as I walk in through the gate
He bring out the encyclopaedia
He fire the questions loud and clear
'Who were the Hottentots
what is the capital of Venezuela
and who was the wife of Lot?'
I have to stop and find the answer
Before going into the house
I am turning the pages
With tears running down my face
If I find the answers quickly
There might be some grace
I have to be sure of the spelling
Daddy complaining that I'm not willing
That first year in grammar school
I came second in the class
Daddy want to give me a beating
He says I didn't work hard enough
That the boy who come first must work harder
Now he supervise all my homework
And he make sure I read the newspaper
He says no child of his
Will be allowed to shirk

On Sundays I have to dress in my best
For Sunday school and for church
And as I turned eleven
I gave my heart to the Lord
And became a full member, baptised
I started teaching in the Sunday school
I started to sing in the choir

I read the lesson in the main service
And I now take communion
I drink the wine and eat the bread
They say I'm a shining example
On Friday evenings
There's Youth fellowship
And my friend and I meet in the churchyard
We rehearse for a concert each month
To raise funds for our activities
And I'm known for reciting the poems

The morning I was baptised
All of us dressed in full white
The church made its way to the sea
Which was shining in the sunlight
Pastor Greaves held me firmly
And dipped me three time
Father, son, holy spirit
As I felt the calmness descend
The choir was singing 'Come into my heart'
And I thought I could make a new start
I thought of forgiving my father
As the elders dried me off in the sun
That Sunday I had to testify loud
And I raised my voice to the ceiling
But it wasn't long before I was tempted
By the music playing outside
I couldn't resist mento yard
Mento music was sweet
Mento music was pure
Mento music was turning to reggae
Mento music surrounded the house
The banjo kept time
With the bass rhumba box
And the drummer provided the pulse
I listened from my bedroom each night
And danced to the pull of the moon
So Sunday was Christian
And white as the snow
Friday and Saturday were sin
Some nights I crept out of the house
Risking the wrath of my father
Risking the hurt of my mother

But the mento pulled me round the corner
And my waistline rotated full circle
While my bottom swung side to side
My feet raised the dust
While my pelvis played lust
And I moved from partner to partner
I could hear Granny Sheba
Singing in my head
Come, come, chile
Let we sing the song again
This time we going to dance
We going to dance through sun and rain
We going to dance till all we laughter
Ease away the pain
We going to laugh until the nation
Think we gone insane
So run, come, chile
Let we sing the song again
And the church could not compete
With the mento beat
And in the evening heat, one day
The dancers start compete
I steal out through the door
Cause I want to dance some more
I picked my favourite partner
And went up on the stage
They give us all a number
And the music start to rage
The mento band begin to play
They play through all the figures
I dance the first four
With my back straight, straight
Just waiting for the fifth
When I could release myself from stress
And let go my hips and waist
I wish that Granny Sheba was here
For she would understand
That the dance was in my blood
That the rhythm was in my head
I won the dance that night
The judges picked me out
And as I climbed up
To receive my prize

I saw my father arrive
He pulled me off the stage
And he let go all his rage
And the people at the front
They begged for me
They said don't beat her, father
She is our very best dancer
You should be proud of her
For she has won the prize
And we're sending her to enter the national festival
That calmed him down
Though he still wore a frown
And he marched me home to my mother

It was then I started writing
For the school magazine
Poems about death and the island
My English teacher from Oxford
Said I must have read Dante's *Inferno*
But it was my dreams I was writing
I had such a great fear of dying
A greater fear of losing my mother
What would I do
With my father alone
What would I do
With my mother gone
That thought sent me to church every Sunday
Where I prayed with all of my heart
And made a promise to the Lord
That I would never forget Him
I would always give praise
I would give thanks each day for my mother

The year I turned fourteen
I entered the fourth form
My parents were concerned about exams
And they sent me to board with my form master
He was of English stock
And in Jamaica on contract
With an Irish wife
And a son called David
I lived with them on the school compound
I'm sure my parents weren't worried

That I'd be molested
But that is exactly what happened
He came to my room every night
While his wife snored next door
And played with my body like music
I felt like I was the guilty one
For I enjoyed it and thought it was fun
It reminded me of my childhood
All the games I used to play
He became my first love and I was jealous
I wondered why his wife never suspected
So I kept the secret with him
And when I turned fifteen
After the touching and teasing
He took me all the way
No more was it just play
And I became a woman too early

If only I could tell the truth
Tell the truth to someone
Trapped in my own head and heart
No one to tell
No way to start
I begged my mother to come back home
And that was how it ended
Now my best friend
My best friend
Ronie Russell is pregnant
Ronie who walked
Like she couldn't open her legs
Ronie who never talked to the boys
Ronie whose skirt was longer than ours
Ronie Russell was pregnant
I thanked the Lord it wasn't me
I surely had learnt my lesson
The fear that I felt
At such an early age
I couldn't tell anyone
Not Granny Sheba
Not my mother or father
Not anyone of my friends
But babies were in the air that year
His wife was also pregnant

And the jealousy I felt
Helped steel my tongue
I was glad to be home with my mother
Only to find
She was pregnant too
At fifteen I had a baby sister
My father now lived with us permanently
And this time, my only escape
Was to lock myself in the tiny bedroom
And read books till I fell asleep
Early in the morning I walked the baby
And rumour soon spread that she was mine
But the truth in my heart
Held my head high
And soon again I started dating

If ever youth was moulded
If ever youth was spoiled
Look to the hands we layed them in
Look how those hands were soiled

But still I carried the guilt
It was the beginning of my patchwork quilt

Colour had suddenly beguiled us
And afros were sprouting thick
Nina Simone sang
'Young, gifted and black'
Angela Davis was a hero
And suddenly race
Came into our world
And cities invaded the country
Grandmother Sheba had told me
Of a man called Marcus Garvey
Who preached we should go back to Africa
She laughed and she said
She would have to send Papa Fred
And she would go back to England
For the first time I questioned
Where would I go
I would have to stay in Jamaica
And I saw myself in the eyes of the world
On an island surrounded by water
The sun ripened beaches

The rivers and rocks
The blue clouded mountains
My hair wet, in locks
And I claimed my Arawak heritage
I belonged to this island
I belonged to the bush
All my senses were wakened around me
That was the year of the black power rally
The year of our new consciousness
And as I was head girl at the moment
I was expected to give an address
I prepared a speech on our nation
A speech on how Jamaica was born
A speech of peasants and workers together
Making the revolution
But as the morning came up bright and early
My deputy came over to me
And said the committee had decided
That I was too white to speak
The hurt that I felt
Followed me for years
I took refuge in Granny Sheba's songs
Which I now knew were the folk songs of our people
The songs which were born on our land

And I remembered the stories
Of Granny Sheba
Of women who begat
Like in Genesis
All I wanted then was my own family
So I married the first man
Who asked for my hand
As soon as I finished 'A' Levels
I was barely seventeen
And I lived in a dream
I married my geography teacher
And my father whispered in my ear
As I walked with him up the aisle
'I shall be walking up this aisle
With a liability on my arm
And walking back down without it'
I took it for his sense of humour
I looked at my mother and cried

Not knowing why tears came into my eyes
But I had taken him up to Hillside
Where he remembered his homeland of Wales
And he fit in so well
He resembled them all
And our first son seemed to be from Hillside

My marriage didn't last very long
The wildness of bush
And the passion of songs
Kept me out dancing all night
With lovers on the left
And lovers on the right
I did not even think it was wrong
I just tumbled along
Letting life take me where it led me
So I gave up my teaching that year
And worked with the arts in the community
Preparing groups to mark the festivities
Of ten years of independence
I grew with Jamaica into a new nation
Proud of our youth and development
It was then life dealt me a blow
That no young adult should know
I was driving musicians
To a concert
When a child ran out on the road
That meeting of metal and blood
As I lifted the child from the ground
Was something I'd never forget
And the voices of shock
Started ringing in my head
And I wrote my new songs to the dead
Those poems I had to destroy
They were too painful to carry so far
And I walked out of home
Out of family
And took to the streets instead
I walked all the way to Hillside
To the funeral of Papa Fred
And Granny Sheba held me
And rocked me in her arms
Life would never be the same again

The songs of joy were now filled with pain
The poems I wrote had become frightening
Death, bush and blood
Took over my rhymes
I was tried in the court for manslaughter
But was found innocent of the crime
Immediately after I left home for Kingston
And entered the school of drama
I found I couldn't put down my pen
It was a year that fulfilled all my yearning
I could forget myself on the stage
And that summer I toured round the island
And my stories filled page after page

It was then I found my second love
A Rastafarian who lived in the hills
On the eastern side of the island
The other side from where I had lived
We looked like brother and sister
Many thought we were family
But my father refused to accept it
And when we visited home
He took out the dictionary
And said to look up the meaning of dread
For that is what you have become
It was what they called Rastafarians
And he would not give us any welcome
It means terrible, frightening, horrible
You are no daughter of mine

That year I got pregnant again
And at the time I was due
I decided to go home to my mother
So my son would be there too
I wanted him to know the baby
And not to feel left out by me
My father's face filled with anger
But he was weak and seemed very old
And late one night
When my mother was called out
My baby's father arrived
I went to wake up my father
To tell him the visitors were mine

I found him dead in the toilet
I was filled with fright and went cold
I felt the child in my belly
And got scared that she too would go
My mother came home
And the house filled
With neighbours that she had called
But Granny Sheba arrived the next morning
And took me to stay in Hillside
It was there that the pains started coming
It was there that my second child was born
And I hugged her with my son beside me
And sung them Granny Sheba's songs

Three weeks later I left with her father
And went back to the hills in the east
Back to a mountain's isolation
And that's where new voices began

One evening
One evening
One evening when the fire burst
When the fire burst in the bamboo roots
And it was the fireflies
It was the fireflies I remembered
And the dark descending
The Rastafarian drumming
That had calmed me for so long
The slow repeating drumbeats
The voices raised in song
That evening they grew louder
As the bamboo fire burst
My head seemed to split open with them
And the memories of death overflowed
I had the new child in my arms
And I started walking
Her father tried to take her back
And I started screaming
I screamed out 'Jah'
I screamed out 'Jah'
I screamed out 'Jah Rastafari'
But no answer came to me
So I continued walking

I walked the five miles through the bush
Down to the nearest road
I took a bus to the train station
The cheapest way to get back home
I would find my way back to my mother
Where I could get some rest
All the way drums filled my head
The train played its own music
I held my daughter close to me
So close I felt her heartbeat
And all I could remember
Was the accident
And holding the dead child to me
Everywhere I went
I prayed as the train rocked me
Please don't take my child away
Please don't take my child away
But the voices said they'd take her
They'd take my child away

Late that night, I arrived
Back in Mosquito Cove
My mother cried when she saw me
And gently freed the child
She tucked me into bed that night
And for a while I felt quite safe
But then I heard my father's voice
Telling me to leave
I woke up screaming
Grabbed the child
And ran out into the road
My mother woke
Came after me
And finally talked me home
But from then on, every night,
I started walking the streets
Carrying my daughter with me
Cursing at strangers and hitching rides
But not going anywhere
And breaking my mother's heart

She finally got me to a doctor
Who diagnosed schizophrenia

And kept me for a month in hospital
Medicating and tying me down
As I tried to jump through the window
To get back to my child

Breaking up is never easy
And now I had done it again
I was the mother of two children
With different fathers who were both absent
But my first husband came on a visit
And my son burst out crying as he left
I said would you like to be with him
And the light in his eyes answered that
So my son went to live with his father
And I stayed home with my mother
Trying to look after his sister
And I began writing again

The voices that visited me
Sometimes would tell a story
That was easy to write
That would shed some light
But soon came the ones that would pain me
I would turn on the radio to soothe me
And do whatever the radio said
So the reggae entered my veins
The drums of mento and rastafari
Joined up in every refrain
I sat still and listened to the lyrics
And this song played over and over again
'Sitting on the dock of the bay,
Waiting for you'
It went over and over again in my head
Waiting for you
Waiting for you
And I grabbed my mother and kissed her
And handed her my daughter
I rushed out of the house
To Montego Bay
Where there was the only dock that I knew
I took with me pen and paper
So I would have something to do
While I waited, I wrote

What I wrote, I sang
And a Rastaman walked over to me
And asked if I was a poet
The next week, he said, there was a stage show
To mark Haile Selassie's birthday
Come, sistren, and chant some lyrics for us
I looked at him, locks longer than mine,
They were grey, which made him an elder
I felt most humble and honoured
And the following week
I chanted my poems
In the amphitheatre

The stage became my home
The poems were my dance
It seemed like everytime I wrote
I would go into a trance
And I heard myself on the radio
And I travelled round the land
Giving voice to the lyrics
And singing Granny Sheba's songs

Then the invitation came
To perform in England
Granny Sheba was excited
She went through the family tree
And told me the names to search for
That would lead them back to me

England crept over me, cold
Descending from sun, through the clouds
Over houses that breathed out smoke
London city so new yet so old
I arrived in the middle of Brixton
Filled with West Indian life
And met people like me from other islands
Trinidadians, Grenadians and Bajans
All celebrating where they had come from
It seemed futile to try and trace family
From the accident of our names
Instead I told tales of Jamaica
And brought mento and reggae to the stage
What a welcome I received there

So I decided to stay
It was there I met my third lover
Who reminded me of Papa Fred
Blacker than my father
From the island of Grenada
And I became Caribbean

The years passed between Jamaica and England
But there was one thing I hadn't fulfilled
I wanted to go to Africa
And I wanted my children with me
After years of chanting Rastafari
I did not want to travel alone
Because I thought I might stay there
I might find Africa to be home
But that year I found myself pregnant again
And my third child arrived in Brixton
Black like her father
Beautiful black
Completing my rainbow of children
And when she was old enough
I accepted an invitation to Africa
I took my three children with me
On what became a frightening journey

I arrived in Johannesburg
With what my mother called
My very own patchwork quilt
Three children of different colours
What Hillside had taken five generations to do
I had done in one
So I arrived on the continent of Africa
But it was not as I had imagined
Joburg was like any other city
Generous and jealous at once
My friends had told me to kiss the earth
As soon as I got there
But there was only concrete
And that didn't seem the same
I gathered my children around me
Wondering if I was at home
But the voices of imminent death
Came back and filled up my head

I did not know who to turn to
I was scared for my children as well
They had gone out for a walk in a park
And had not returned when they should have done
My hosts filled me with stories of crime
That filled my heart with fear
I started searching through the streets
And screaming out their names
Then I knew I was further from home
Than I had ever been in my life
The feeling of being in a foreign land
Where the colours still hated each other
What if I lost my children here
What if death played its hand

By the time we found the children
My mind had already broken
They brought me doctors
They brought me herbal healers
They brought me a soothsayer
But all I could do
Was get on the plane
And take my children back to England
Back to England
Back to hospital
But at least it was familiar
When I got well I was sure of one thing
That the island of Jamaica was home
That we belonged to that little island
I was glad I had travelled
But there was no search in me anymore
You never knew just where you had come from
Until you ventured out on your own

The poems and songs of Jamaica
Had taken me all round the world
But my journey with me rainbow children
Had taken me back to Hillside
Where Granny Sheba was ailing
Where all my relatives had lived and died
It was home like there was no other
Where everyone knew who we were
And when the women saw my third child

They said she was my father's tribe
So the four of us settled into Hillside
Where all the tribes could now be found
I spent my time
Nursing Granny Sheba
Not wanting her to die
Then she called me in one morning
And said that the house was mine
That day she asked me to cook for her
Her favourite curried goat and rice
And then she asked me to bathe her
With bushes from round Hillside
She said she had read in the Bible
That anywhere you were born
The Lord had put herbs round about you
You would be cured from your own land
So I bathed her and dressed her gently
In the lavender night gown she loved
And she went to bed that evening
And slept and never woke
Early the next morning I found her
When I brought in her tea
I wept silently
Then gathered myself
And prepared to honour her parting
For she was my roots
Hillside my birthplace
And neither England nor Africa
Could replace the history she'd given
All the stories she had told me
All the songs that she had sung

Hillside is no longer
The back of beyond
An hour's drive through the valley is an airport
I fly round the world with my poems
I fly round the world with my songs
But I always return to Hillside
For that is where I belong
And when the voices disturb me
When death seems to take over my pen
I sit quietly mongst the mahoe trees
And sing Granny Sheba's songs

Come, come chile
Let we sing the song again
And this time we going to dance
We going to dance through sun and rain
We going to dance until we laughter
Wear out all the pain
We going to laugh until the nation
Think we gone insane
So come, come chile
Let we sing the song again